BECAUSE WE ARE
CALLED TO

COUNTER
CULTURE

IN A WORLD OF

POVERTY · SAME-SEX MARRIAGE · RACISM

SEX SLAVERY · IMMIGRATION · PERSECUTION

ABORTION · ORPHANS · PORNOGRAPHY

DAVID PLATT

✒ TYNDALE HOUSE PUBLISHERS, INC., CAROL STREAM, ILLINOIS

Visit Tyndale online at www.tyndale.com.

TYNDALE and Tyndale's quill logo are registered trademarks of Tyndale House Publishers, Inc.

Because We Are Called to Counter Culture: In a World of Poverty, Same-Sex Marriage, Racism, Sex Slavery, Immigration, Persecution, Abortion, Orphans, and Pornography

Copyright © 2015 by David Platt. All rights reserved.

Designed by Dean H. Renninger

ISBN 978-1-4964-0533-3 (sampler). Order full product under ISBN 978-1-4143-7329-4.

Printed in the United States of America

21	20	19	18	17	16	15
7	6	5	4	3	2	1

COUNTERING CULTURE

Imagine standing at the height of all the earth and seeing the depth of human poverty.

Journey with me to the middle of the Himalayan mountains, where not long ago I met men and women striving for survival. Half the children in these particular villages die before their eighth birthday. Many don't make it to their first. Meet Radha, a mom who would have fourteen kids if twelve of them hadn't died before adulthood. Meet Kunsing, a disabled child who spent the first twelve years of his life chained in a barn because his family thought he was cursed. Meet Chimie, a toddler whose brother and sister died when he was two months old, leading his mom to commit suicide and his dad to pass him around desperately to any woman in the village who could provide nourishment.

Just as shocking as those you meet are those you don't. Some of the villages in these mountains are virtually devoid of young girls between the ages of five and fifteen. Their parents were persuaded by the promises of a better life for their daughters, so they sent them off with men who turned out to be traffickers. Most of these girls live to see their eighth birthday, but by their sixteenth birthday they are forced to have sex with thousands of customers. They will never see their families again.

When we meet people, hear stories, and see faces of injustice like this around the world, it is altogether right for us to respond with compassion, conviction, and courage. Compassion overwhelms us because we care deeply for children, parents, and families whose lives are filled with pain and suffering. Conviction overtakes us, for every one of us knows instinctively that stories like these should not be so. It is not right for half the children in these Himalayan villages to die before their eighth birthday. It is not fair for children born with disabilities to be chained in barns for their entire lives. It is unjust for pimps to deceive parents into selling their precious daughters as sex slaves. Ultimately, such compassion and conviction fuel courage—courage to do something, *anything*, for the sake of Radha, Kunsing, Chimie, these girls, their parents, their villages, and countless other children, women, and men like them around the world.

In light of these global realities, I am greatly encouraged when I see such compassion, conviction, and courage in the church today. As I listen to the way contemporary

Christians talk (especially, though not exclusively, younger evangelicals), I perceive fierce opposition to injustice regarding the poor, the orphan, and the enslaved. I observe increased awareness of social issues: a plethora of books written, conferences organized, and movements started that revolve around fighting hunger, alleviating poverty, and ending sex trafficking. In the middle of it all, I sense deep dissatisfaction with indifference in the church. We simply aren't content with a church that turns a blind eye and a deaf ear to the realities of social injustice in the world. We want our lives—and the church—to count for social justice.

Yet while I'm deeply encouraged by the expressed zeal of so many Christians for certain social issues, I'm profoundly concerned by the lack of zeal among these same Christians (especially, though again not exclusively, younger evangelicals) for other social issues. On popular issues like poverty and slavery, where Christians are likely to be applauded for our social action, we are quick to stand up and speak out. Yet on controversial issues like homosexuality and abortion, where Christians are likely to be criticized for our involvement, we are content to sit down and stay quiet. It's as if we've decided to pick and choose which social issues we'll contest and which we'll concede. And our picking and choosing normally revolves around what is most comfortable—and least costly—for us in our culture.

If you ask practically any popular Christian leader in the public square to make a statement on poverty, sex trafficking, or the orphan crisis, that leader will gladly, boldly, and clearly share his or her convictions. However, if you ask the same Christian leader in the same public setting to make a statement on homosexuality or abortion, that leader will respond with either nervous hesitancy or virtual heresy, if he or she responds at all. "That's not the issue I'm concerned with," the leader might say. "My focus is on this other issue, and that's what I want to speak about."

The practical effect of this is evident across the contemporary Christian landscape. All sorts of younger evangelicals write blogs, take pictures, send tweets, and attend conferences where they fight to alleviate poverty and end slavery. Other evangelicals care for foster children in the United States and adopt orphans from around the world. Many of these efforts are good, and we should continue in them. What is problematic, however, is when these same evangelicals stay silent in conversations about more culturally controversial issues like abortion or so-called same-sex marriage. *Those issues are not my concern,* they think. *I'm more comfortable talking about other issues.*

But what if Christ commands us to make these issues our concern? And what if Christ's call in our lives is not to comfort in our culture? What if Christ in us actually compels us to counter our culture? Not to quietly sit and watch evolving cultural trends and not to subtly shift our views amid changing cultural tides, but to courageously share and show our convictions through what we say and how we live, even (or especially) when these convictions contradict the popular positions of our day. And to do all of this not with conceited minds or calloused hearts, but with the humble compassion of Christ on constant display in everything we say and do.

Isn't this, after all, the essence of what it means to follow Christ in the first place? "If anyone would come after me, let him deny himself and take up his cross daily and follow me" (Luke 9:23). Talk about countercultural. In a world where everything revolves around yourself—protect yourself, promote yourself, comfort yourself, and take care of yourself— Jesus says, "Crucify yourself. Put aside all self-preservation in order to live for God's glorification, no matter what that means for you in the culture around you."

And isn't this, after all, the main issue in any culture? Maybe better stated, isn't *he* the main issue in any culture? What if the main issue in our culture today is not poverty or sex trafficking, homosexuality or abortion? What if the main issue is *God*? And what might happen if we made *him* our focus instead? In a world marked by sex slavery and sexual immorality, the abandonment of children and the murder of children, racism and persecution, the needs of the poor and the neglect of the widow, how would we act if we fixed our gaze on the holiness, love, goodness, truth, justice, authority, and mercy of God revealed in the gospel?

These are the questions driving me, and I invite you to explore them with me. I don't by any means claim to know all the answers. But I've got this sense that if we take an honest look at our lives, our families, and our churches, we may realize that much of our supposed social justice is actually a selective social injustice. We may recognize that what we thought were separate social issues are in fact all intimately connected to our understanding of who God is and what God is doing in the world. In the process, we may find that the same heart of God that moves us to war against sex trafficking also moves us to war against sexual immorality. We may discover that the same gospel that compels us to combat poverty also compels us to defend marriage. And in the end, we may resolve to rearrange our lives, families, and churches around a more consistent, Christ-compelled, countercultural response to the most pressing social issues of our day.

Inevitably, God will lead us to act in different ways. Not every one of us can give equal attention to all the issues I've described. No one can fight sex trafficking while fostering and adopting children in the middle of starting a ministry for widows and counseling unwed mothers while traveling around the world to support the persecuted church— and so on. Nor *should* any one of us do all these things, for God sovereignly puts us in unique positions and places with unique privileges and opportunities to influence the culture around us. But what is necessary for all of us is to view each of these cultural issues through the lens of biblical truth and to speak such truth with conviction whenever we have the chance to do so. Then, based on consistent conviction, we seek how individually as Christians and collectively in our churches the Spirit of Christ is leading us to compassionate action in our culture.

In order to help us in this, I've offered some initial suggestions for practical requests you and I can pray in light of these issues, potential ways you or I might engage culture with the gospel, and biblical truths we must proclaim regarding every one of these issues. These suggestions will also point you to a website where you can explore more specific steps you might take. I encourage you to consider all these suggestions and to humbly, boldly, seriously, and prayerfully consider what God is directing you to do. Let's not merely contemplate the Word of God in the world around us; let's do what it says (see James 1:22-25).

To be sure, what we conclude about countering culture may prove costly for you and me. But by that point, I don't think this will matter much. For our eyes will no longer be focused on what is most comfortable to us; instead, our lives will be fixed on what is most glorifying to God, and in him we will find far greater reward than anything our culture could ever offer us.

POVERTY

When I traveled through a series of snow-covered Asian villages, I saw what happens when severe poverty turns simple illness into almost certain death. We met people and heard stories of men, women, and children who had died or were dying of preventable diseases. One village we passed had recently experienced a cholera outbreak. Up to sixty people had died in a matter of weeks because of a simple stomach infection due to impure water and poor hygiene. In case you read quickly over that last sentence, that's a huge portion of an entire community who died of diarrhea.

On the same day I was walking through these villages, I read in Luke 10 Jesus' summary of all God's commandments to his people: "You shall love the Lord your God with all your heart and with all your soul and with all your strength and with all your mind, and your neighbor as yourself" (verse 27). That last phrase jumped off the page in light of the picture I was seeing. "Love your neighbor as yourself."

As myself?

I wondered what I would want someone to do for me if I lived in one of these villages. Wouldn't I want somebody to help me? Or what if it were my kids or the children in my church dying of preventable diseases? What if *half* your children or my children were dying before they turned eight? If this were us, or if this were our kids, or if this were the children in our churches, we would do something.

Ignoring such urgent needs simply would not be an option.

Yet this is exactly what so many of us in the Western church have done. We have insulated and isolated ourselves from the massive material poverty that surrounds us in the world. We have filled our lives and our churches with more comforts for us, all while turning a blind eye and a deaf ear to abject poverty in others. We need our eyes opened to the implications of the gospel for how we live.

PRAY

Ask God to:

- Intervene on behalf of the poor, both close to home and around the world.
- Soften your heart to identify with the poor and work for their good.
- Reveal ways that you can live on less

in order to give more to those who need it.

PARTICIPATE

Prayerfully consider taking these steps:

- Investigate local ministries that are involved in serving the poor in your community, and ask how you or your church body can partner with them.
- Look at your budget. Are there any luxuries you can sacrifice in order to have more resources to give to those in need?
- Make a list of your talents and assets, and consider the global needs you are aware of. Is there any place where your resources and the world's needs intersect?

PROCLAIM

Consider the following truths from Scripture:

- Acts 20:35, NIV: "In everything I did, I showed you that by this kind of hard work we must help the weak, remembering the words the Lord Jesus himself said: 'It is more blessed to give than to receive.'"
- 2 Corinthians 8:9: "You know the grace of our Lord Jesus Christ, that though he was rich, yet for your sake he became poor, so that you by his poverty might become rich."
- 1 John 3:17: "If anyone has the world's goods and sees his brother in need, yet closes his heart against him, how does God's love abide in him?"

For more (and more specific) suggestions, visit CounterCultureBook.com/Poverty.

ABORTION

Across the world, more than forty-two million abortions occur every year. That's 115,000 abortions every single day. I find it hard to fathom that number when I look at the faces of my four children each night as I put them to bed. I find it hard to imagine 115,000 other children who that day were introduced to the world with a tool or pill aimed at taking their lives. And I find it hardest to comprehend how I, for so long, could show no concern for this gruesome global reality.

Abortion is without question an assault on God's grand creation of a human life. There is no way around it. Our lives and language testify to this. I remember the pure joy when we found out that my wife, Heather, was pregnant. From the very beginning, we talked about our son like he was a person. He was never a clump of tissue that could become our son if we chose to have him. He was our child from the start, and we loved him as such.

My wife and I are not alone in this. Even abortion advocates join with us, albeit unintentionally, in talking about unborn babies as exactly that: *babies*. I remember when reports announced that Prince William and his wife, Kate, were expecting their first child. Even the most secular news outlets immediately began talking about the child in the womb as an heir to the throne. They made much of the significance of this baby, and no one spoke in terms of a "blastocyst" or "blob of cells." We would loathe the journalist who dared to use such language. But doesn't the dignity we conferred on a "royal" baby apply also to countless other "ordinary" babies whose lives are no less significant?

PRAY

Ask God to:

- End the injustice of abortion in our country and around the world.
- Forgive you for whatever part you have played in abortion—even silence.
- Convict those in positions of power to use their influence to end abortion.

PARTICIPATE

Prayerfully consider taking these steps:

- Write to your representatives in Congress and clearly and respectfully lay out why abortion in this country must stop.
- Work with ministries or participate in events (e.g., Sanctity of Human

Life Sunday, 40 Days for Life, prayer walks) that seek to uphold the value of unborn human life.

- Volunteer with a crisis pregnancy center in your city to aid in their work of showing women in desperate situations that there are options other than abortion.

PROCLAIM

Consider the following truths from Scripture:

- Psalm 139:15-16: "My frame was not hidden from you, when I was being made in secret, intricately woven in the depths of the earth. Your eyes saw my unformed substance; in your book were written, every one of them, the days that were formed for me, when as yet there was none of them."
- Proverbs 24:10-12: "If you faint in the day of adversity, your strength is

small. Rescue those who are being taken away to death; hold back those who are stumbling to the slaughter. If you say, 'Behold, we did not know this,' does not he who weighs the heart perceive it? Does not he who keeps watch over your soul know it, and will he not repay man according to his work?"

- Matthew 19:14: "Jesus said, 'Let the little children come to me and do not hinder them, for to such belongs the kingdom of heaven.'"

For more (and more specific) suggestions, visit CounterCultureBook.com/Abortion.

ORPHANS AND WIDOWS

When you read the Bible, you see over and over God's passion to demonstrate his power and love in the life of orphans and widows. "The LORD your God is God of gods and Lord of lords, the great, the mighty, and the awesome God, who is not partial and takes no bribe. He executes justice for the fatherless and the widow" (Deuteronomy 10:17-18). "Father of the fatherless and protector of widows is God in his holy habitation" (Psalm 68:5). Continually throughout their history, God exhorts his people, "Learn to do good; seek justice, correct oppression; bring justice

to the fatherless, plead the widow's cause"
(Isaiah 1:17).

We live in the midst of an orphan crisis.
Approximately 153 million children live as
orphans, meaning they have lost at least one
parent. Included in that number are about 18
million children who have lost both parents.
Not included in that number, though, are
the millions of effectively orphaned children
who live in institutions or on the streets, in
addition to vast multitudes who live as "social orphans," meaning that even if a parent
is alive, the children rarely, if ever, see that
parent or experience life as part of a family.

More than that, orphans and widows
often live in the same home. When Scripture
speaks of the orphan and the widow, doubt-
less it refers primarily to those who were
orphaned or widowed due to a parent's or
husband's death. But at the present time, well
over a third of children in the United States

are living in a home with only one parent, and nearly half of all births are to unmarried women—both inevitable realities in a culture that minimizes the priority and permanence of marriage. The result is a growing number of children and women who lack a parent or husband in the home.

The implications of this are mammoth for the church in contemporary culture. Now, possibly more than at any other point in history, the church has an opportunity to rise up and show God's love not just to children and women whose parents or husbands have died but also to children and women whose parents or husbands have disappeared from their lives. Christ compels us to counter culture by stepping in to care for orphans and widows when significant people have stepped out of their lives. Indeed, the Father to the fatherless and the Defender of the widow is calling his people to care for these children and women as our own families.

PRAY
Ask God to:
- Open your eyes to see the orphans and widows around you.
- Empower Christians around the world to protect the most vulnerable.
- Remind you of the way he has adopted you as his child in Christ.

PARTICIPATE
Prayerfully consider taking these steps:
- Start the process of foster care or adoption, or find tangible ways to support families who are fostering or adopting children.
- Either on your own or with your family, consider reaching out to, spending time with, and serving a

specific orphan or widow in your church or neighborhood.

- Sponsor an orphan or widow in another country through a gospel-driven Christian ministry and maintain contact with the person you are sponsoring.

PROCLAIM

Consider the following truths from Scripture:

- Psalm 68:5-6: "Father of the fatherless and protector of widows is God in his holy habitation. God settles the solitary in a home."
- Galatians 4:4-5: "When the fullness of time had come, God sent forth his Son, born of woman, born under the law, to redeem those who were under the law, so that we might receive adoption as sons."
- James 1:27: "Religion that is pure and

undefiled before God, the Father, is this: to visit orphans and widows in their affliction, and to keep oneself unstained from the world."

For more (and more specific) suggestions, visit CounterCultureBook.com/Orphans andWidows.

SEX SLAVERY

I am ashamed to confess that it wasn't until recently that I realized the severity of sex trafficking in the world around me. For a long time, the idea of slavery seemed to me a relic of a bygone era centuries before my time. I never could have imagined that there are more slaves today than were seized from Africa in four centuries of the transatlantic slave trade. I never could have comprehended that twenty-seven million people live in slavery today—more than at any other time in history. I never could have fathomed that many of these millions are being bought, sold, and exploited for sex in what has become one of the fastest-growing industries on earth.

But even when I heard these numbers, they still seemed distant to me. As long as they were mere numbers on a page, I could insulate and isolate myself from them. Quite honestly, I could live as if they didn't exist—both the numbers and the individuals they represent.

That all changed when I walked through a village in the Nupri valley of Nepal. For the first time in my life, I came face-to-face with the horrifying reality of what happens in those mountains. I heard story after story of girl after girl, and when I got back to the big city of Kathmandu, I walked past restaurant after restaurant with slaves waiting outside to provide services in cubicles inside. I saw where these girls once lived, and I saw where these girls now work, and no matter how hard I try, I can't get these sights out of my mind.

When I flew back from Nepal, I landed in Atlanta and drove along Interstate 20 to my home in Birmingham. I have grown up going up and down this interstate that spans all the way to west Texas, and I had no idea that it is the "sex-trafficking superhighway" of the United States. This same road that represents freedom for ten million travelers every year reflects the reality of slavery for countless girls every night. It changes your perspective to realize that the man and young woman at the table next to you at the rest stop may not be what you once thought.

Slavery still exists. And now that I know it does, I have no choice but to do something about it. Further, now that *you* know it does, you have no choice but to do something about it.

PRAY

Ask God to:

- Intervene and rescue individuals around the world who are being used as sex slaves.
- Open the eyes of Christians and churches to the plight of sex slaves.
- Redeem the perpetrators of sex slavery or otherwise execute justice in light of their sin.

PARTICIPATE

Prayerfully consider taking these steps:

- Support a ministry that addresses the problem of sex slavery and consider ways you can be involved in their work.
- Make fellow church members or church leaders aware of this issue so that you can pray for the victims of

sex slavery and strategize how to help them.
- Call and write to your government representatives urging them to oppose sex trafficking as well as the pornography industry.

PROCLAIM

Consider the following truths from Scripture:
- Psalm 24:1 (NIV): "The earth is the LORD's, and everything in it, the world, and all who live in it."
- Psalm 82:4: "Rescue the weak and the needy; deliver them from the hand of the wicked."
- Psalm 7:11: "God is a righteous judge, and a God who feels indignation every day."

For more (and more specific) suggestions, visit CounterCultureBook.com/SexSlavery.

MARRIAGE

From the beginning of time, God designed marriage for a purpose. That purpose was not fully revealed until Jesus died on the cross, rose from the dead, and instituted the church. After all of this, the Bible looks back to the institution of marriage and asserts, "This mystery [of marriage] is profound, and . . . it refers to Christ and the church" (Ephesians 5:32). When God made man, then woman, and then brought them together in a relationship called marriage, he wasn't simply rolling dice, drawing straws, or flipping a coin. He was painting a picture.

His intent from the start was to illustrate his love for people.

Unfortunately, this is not the picture of marriage that the world most often perceives. And the primary reason is not the laws in various states, or the decision of judicial bodies to redefine what marriage is. The primary reason the gospel is not clear in marriage in our culture is that the gospel has not been clear in marriage in the church. Surely personal, not political, action is the primary starting point to counter culture in this area.

It is altogether right to be grieved about the redefinition of marriage in our culture. So-called "same-sex marriage" is now recognized as a legitimate entity in the eyes of our government. Such a designation by a government, however, does not change the definition God has established. And as spiritual darkness engulfs the biblical picture of marriage in our culture, spiritual light will stand out even more starkly in the portrait of a husband who lays down his life for his wife and a wife who joyfully follows her husband's loving leadership. Be sure of this: God's design for marriage is far more breathtaking and much more satisfying than anything we could ever create on our own.

PRAY

Ask God to:

- Empower you to be pure, faithful, and selfless in your own marriage or in your singleness.
- Strengthen the church's witness to the beauty of the gospel and to the biblical pattern of marriage.
- Change the hearts and minds of legislative and judicial bodies on the issue of so-called same-sex marriage.

PARTICIPATE

Prayerfully consider taking these steps:

- Humbly ask the leadership of your church to address the topic of marriage through the preaching and/or teaching ministries of the church.
- Offer to talk to, pray with, or meet with individuals you know (of the same gender) who are struggling in their marriage.
- Vote for political candidates who support a biblical view of marriage and actively encourage them to continue their support.

PROCLAIM

Consider the following truths from Scripture:

- Genesis 2:24: "A man shall leave his father and his mother and hold fast to his wife, and they shall become one flesh."

- Ephesians 5:22, 25: "Wives, submit to your own husbands, as to the Lord. . . . Husbands, love your wives, as Christ loved the church and gave himself up for her."
- Hebrews 13:4: "Let marriage be held in honor among all, and let the marriage bed be undefiled, for God will judge the sexually immoral and adulterous."

For more (and more specific) suggestions, visit CounterCultureBook.com/Marriage.

SEXUAL MORALITY

God prohibits sexual worship—the idolization of sex and infatuation with sexual activity as a fundamental means to personal fulfillment. All throughout Scripture and history, people have mistakenly fallen into the trap of thinking that the God-created pleasure of sex and sexuality will bring us ultimate satisfaction (see Exodus 32:2-6; Deuteronomy 23:17; Proverbs 7:1-27; 1 Corinthians 10:8). Sadly, it seems that we are no different in our time. All across our culture, people believe, "If only I have sexual freedom in this way or that way, then I will be happy." But this is not true. Sex is good, but sex is not God. It will not ultimately fulfill. Like anything else that becomes an idol, it will always take more than it gives while diverting the human heart away from the only One who is able to give supreme joy.

Each of the Bible's sexual prohibitions is encapsulated in the all-encompassing command "Flee from sexual immorality" (1 Corinthians 6:18). These words were written to a church in the sex-crazed city of Corinth, where singles were sexually involved before marriage, husbands and wives were sexually involved outside of marriage, homosexuality was condoned, and prostitution was common. (Not much has changed in two thousand years.) So to the church in that culture and to the church in our culture, God says, "Flee from sexual immorality—any and all sexual thinking, looking, desiring, touching, speaking, and acting outside of marriage between a man and a woman.

Don't rationalize it, and don't reason with it—*run from it*. Flee it as fast as you can."

But we don't believe God on this one. None of us do. The Bible doesn't speak simply against adultery or homosexuality but against multiple manifestations of sexual immorality in every single one of our lives. All of us—men and women, heterosexual and homosexual—are sexual sinners, and all of us are in need of a Savior.

PRAY

Ask God to:

- Bring conviction and repentance in the lives of Christians (including you) involved in sexual immorality.
- Give Christians compassion, boldness, wisdom, and humility in addressing issues such as homosexual activity, pornography, and other forms of sexual sin.

- Open the hearts of unbelievers to see that God forgives and breaks the power of sexual sin and that true freedom is found in Jesus Christ.

PARTICIPATE

Prayerfully consider taking these steps:

- Meet with a small group of others in your church to exhort one another to sexual purity and faithfulness.
- Support or become involved in a ministry that helps those who struggle with same-sex attraction.
- Contact government officials and exhort them to enact and implement legislation that will prevent the exploitation of women (through avenues such as pornography or prostitution) in our culture.

PROCLAIM

Consider the following truths from Scripture:

- 1 Corinthians 6:9-10: "Do you not know that the unrighteous will not inherit the kingdom of God? Do not be deceived: neither the sexually immoral, nor idolaters, nor adulterers, nor men who practice homosexuality, nor thieves, nor the greedy, nor drunkards, nor revilers, nor swindlers will inherit the kingdom of God."

- 1 Corinthians 6:18-20: "Flee from sexual immorality. Every other sin a person commits is outside the body, but the sexually immoral person sins against his own body. Or do you not know that your body is a temple of the Holy Spirit within you, whom you have from God? You are not your own, for you were bought with a price. So glorify God in your body."

- Isaiah 1:18: "Come now, let us reason together, says the LORD: though your

sins are like scarlet, they shall be as
white as snow; though they are red like
crimson, they shall become like wool."

For more (and more specific) suggestions, visit
CounterCultureBook.com/SexualMorality.

ETHNICITY

We live in a culture where we are constantly submerged in discussions about race and racism. We have conversations and host forums, sponsor debates and foster dialogues, write articles and give speeches about how to solve racial tension in our culture. But could it be that the gospel not only counters culture on this issue but reshapes the conversation about race altogether?

Consider the starting point in the gospel: the creation of man and woman in the image of God with equal dignity before God. This means that no human being is more or less human than another. All are made in

God's image. It is a lack of trust in this gospel truth that has led to indescribable horrors in human history. Slavery in America, the Holocaust in Germany, the Armenian massacre in Turkey, the genocide in Rwanda, and the Japanese slaughter of six million Koreans, Chinese, Indo-Chinese, Indonesians, and Filipinos all derived from the satanic deception of leaders and citizens who believed that they were intrinsically superior to other types of people. From the first chapter of the Bible, however, this much is clear: all men and women are made in the very likeness of God. The Bible's story line depicts a basic unity behind worldly diversity.

Throughout history Christians have failed to understand how the gospel affects the way we view and love people of different ethnicities. My hope and prayer is that this would not be what historians write concerning the church in our day. The body of Christ is a multicultural citizenry of an otherworldly kingdom. By the sheer grace of God in the gospel, we are compelled to counter selfish pride and ethnic prejudice both in our hearts and in our culture. For this is not the culture to which we ultimately belong. Instead, we are looking forward to the day when "a great multitude that no one [can] number, from every nation, from all tribes and peoples and languages" (Revelation 7:9) will stand as one redeemed race to give glory to the Father who calls us not sojourners or exiles, but sons and daughters.

PRAY

Ask God to:

- Open the eyes of all believers (including your own) to selfish pride and sinful prejudice and to grant repentance.
- Protect and provide for immigrants

and their families and to put believers in their paths to minister to them.

- Give the leadership of the United States (and other governments) wisdom in addressing the issue of immigration.

PARTICIPATE

Prayerfully consider taking these steps:

- Talk with the leadership of your church about partnering in ministry with a church whose members are of a different ethnicity from yours.
- Open your home to someone from a different people group. Consider specifically international students, as the vast majority of these individuals never have an opportunity to go inside the home of an American family.
- Begin a ministry to immigrants in need in your local area. Provide food,

shelter, and help with the language. Most important, proclaim the gospel to them.

PROCLAIM

Consider the following truths from Scripture:

- Acts 17:26: "He made from one man every nation of mankind to live on all the face of the earth, having determined allotted periods and the boundaries of their dwelling place."
- Deuteronomy 10:19: "Love the sojourner, therefore, for you were sojourners in the land of Egypt."
- Galatians 3:28: "There is neither Jew nor Greek, there is neither slave nor free, there is no male and female, for you are all one in Christ Jesus."

For more (and more specific) suggestions, visit CounterCultureBook.com/Ethnicity.

RELIGIOUS LIBERTY

One of the fundamental human freedoms—if not the most fundamental human freedom—is the privilege of each person to explore truth about the divine and to live in light of his or her determinations. Obviously, different people will make different determinations regarding what to believe, whom to worship, and how to live. This is a choice God has offered to all people, for from the beginning God has given men and women the freedom to decide whether to worship him.

Around the world, scores of men and women from many faiths, including many of our brothers and sisters in Christ, live today without this fundamental freedom. Millions of people are presently denied the opportunity to even explore truth that will affect their lives on earth and for eternity.

Government coercion is one of the greatest restrictors of religious liberty around the globe. This is most clear in communist and Islamist states, where countries adopt an official religion (or nonreligion) and require their citizens to conform to corresponding beliefs. Societal pressure follows closely on the heels of governmental regulation as family, friends, religious fanatics, community leaders, and criminal mobs intimidate, threaten, harm, or kill men, women, and children who profess certain faith. Such pressure accounts for much Christian persecution today.

Surrounded by this global reality, and driven by our love for God, we must act. We must pray and work for our persecuted brothers and sisters around the world. When one part of the body suffers, the whole body suffers (see 1 Corinthians 12). Moreover, in a country where even our own religious liberty is increasingly limited, our suffering brothers and sisters beckon us not to let the cost of following Christ in our culture silence our faith.

PRAY

Ask God to:

- Prepare Christians in our own culture to respond boldly and humbly to increased governmental and cultural opposition.
- Work in the lives of rulers in our own country and around the world so that there is more freedom given to live and speak according to the truth of the gospel.
- Strengthen persecuted believers

around the world to persevere in faith and to continue to bear witness to Christ, regardless of the consequences.

PARTICIPATE

Prayerfully consider taking these steps:

- Contact your state government representatives about instances here and abroad where religious liberty is being denied.
- Support and/or get involved with a ministry that speaks on behalf of believers who live in persecuted contexts.
- Consider how you or someone you know might get involved on the issue of religious liberty, either legally or politically.

PROCLAIM

Consider the following truths from Scripture:

- Matthew 5:11-12: "Blessed are you

when others revile you and persecute you and utter all kinds of evil against you falsely on my account. Rejoice and be glad, for your reward is great in heaven."

- Proverbs 21:1: "The king's heart is a stream of water in the hand of the LORD; he turns it wherever he will."
- 1 Peter 2:23: "When [Christ] was reviled, he did not revile in return; when he suffered, he did not threaten, but continued entrusting himself to him who judges justly."

For more (and more specific) suggestions, visit CounterCultureBook.com/ReligiousLiberty.

UNREACHED
PEOPLE GROUPS

Throughout this booklet, we have considered massive physical needs in the world. Yet if we are not careful, we run the risk of ignoring people's most pressing need—the gospel.

Jesus knew that as great as people's earthly needs were, their eternal need was far greater. When a paralytic was brought to him on a mat, Jesus said to him, "Son, your sins are forgiven" (Mark 2:5). He used this opportunity to teach a paralyzed man and the people around him that the ultimate priority of his coming was not to relieve suffering, as important as that is. Instead, his ultimate priority was to sever the root of suffering: sin itself.

Because the gospel is the most pressing need in people's lives, the gospel informs the fundamental purpose of our lives. We who know the gospel have been given the greatest gift in all the world. We have good news of a glorious God who has come to deliver men, women, and children from all sin and all suffering for all time. Therefore, we cannot—we *must* not—stay silent with this gospel. Gospel possession requires gospel proclamation.

The central mission of the church in the world, then, is proclaiming the gospel to the world, and there is much work to be done, not only in our culture but among people around the world. More than six thousand people groups are currently classified as "unreached"—a population of at least two billion people.

When will the concept of unreached peoples become intolerable to the church? What will it take to wake us up to the dearth of the gospel among the peoples of the world? What will it take to stir our hearts and lives for men and women whose souls are plunging into damnation without ever even hearing of salvation? This cannot be conceivable for people who confess the gospel. For if this gospel is true, then we must spend our lives and mobilize our churches for the spread of Christ's love to unreached people groups all around the world. Jesus has not given us a commission to consider; he has given us a command to obey.

PRAY

Ask God to:

- Grant you boldness in proclaiming the gospel to people around you and around the world who don't know Christ.
- Send out workers to other cultures and to open the door for many more

unreached people groups to be reached
with the gospel.

- Give many churches and Christians a
burden to become involved in praying,
giving, and going for the purpose of
taking the gospel to the unreached.

PARTICIPATE

Prayerfully consider taking these steps:

- Give sacrificially through your local
church so that missionaries and gospel
efforts to the unreached might be
supported.
- Plan to go on a short-term mission
trip and ask God to clarify what your
role should be in obeying the great
commission.
- Support a missions agency, a
translation team, or some other effort
to get the gospel to unreached peoples.

PROCLAIM

Consider the following truths from Scripture:

- Matthew 6:9-10: "Our Father in heaven, hallowed be your name. Your kingdom come, your will be done, on earth as it is in heaven."

- Matthew 9:37-38: "[Jesus] said to his disciples, 'The harvest is plentiful, but the laborers are few; therefore pray earnestly to the Lord of the harvest to send out laborers into his harvest.'"

- Luke 24:45-47: "[Jesus] opened their minds to understand the Scriptures, and said to them, 'Thus it is written, that the Christ should suffer and on the third day rise from the dead, and that repentance and forgiveness of sins should be proclaimed in his name to all nations, beginning from Jerusalem.'"

For more (and more specific) suggestions, visit CounterCultureBook.com/Unreached.

ARE *YOU* READY TO
COUNTER CULTURE?

Everywhere we turn, battle lines are being drawn. Seemingly overnight, culture has shifted to the point where right and wrong are no longer measured by universal truth but by popular opinion.

In *Counter Culture*, David Platt shows Christians how to actively take a stand on such issues as poverty, sex trafficking, marriage, abortion, racism, and religious liberty and challenges us to become passionate, unwavering voices for Christ.

Additional study materials are available online and in a bookstore near you. To learn more about how you can counter culture, please visit us at www.counterculturebook.com.

CP0851